MY FIRST CHRISTMAS COOK BOOK

David Atherton

Illustrated by
Katie Cottle

WALKER BOOKS
AND SUBSIDIARIES
LONDON • BOSTON • SYDNEY • AUCKLAND

I love the festive period and spending it with my rock, support and beloved Nik
(also Rey and Kai, too). I couldn't have written this book without my family.

D.A.

For Mum. Thanks for all the dinners (Christmas and otherwise).

K.C.

First published 2023 by Walker Books Ltd, 87 Vauxhall Walk, London SE11 5HJ
10 9 8 7 6 5 4 3 2 1
Text © 2023 Nomadbaker Ltd Illustrations © 2023 Katie Cottle
The Great British Bake Off Baker logo™ is licensed by Love Productions Ltd
The right of David Atherton and Katie Cottle to be identified as author and
illustrator respectively of this work has been asserted in accordance
with the Copyright, Designs and Patents Act 1988
This book has been typeset in Alice and Mrs Ant Printed in China

British Library Cataloguing in Publication Data: a catalogue record for this book
is available from the British Library
ISBN 978-1-5295-0847-5 www.walker.co.uk

All recipes are for informational and/or entertainment purposes only;
please check all ingredients carefully if you have any allergies, and, if in doubt,
consult a health professional. Adult supervision is required for all recipes.

Introduction

At Christmas, it's important to let our family and friends know how much we love them. In a season of giving and sharing, what better way to show them that you care than with a homemade gift? So step into the kitchen and get ready to create beautiful bakes and magical memories to treasure for ever.

In this book, you'll discover recipes to make delicious gifts and stocking fillers, perfect party food and showstopper cakes to share during your Christmas celebrations. Whether you want to impress your friends with an amazing gingerbread house, eat your way through a chocolate Christmas pudding or make a bang with a cracker-shaped cake, this book has everything budding bakers need to get ahead for the festive season.

On a cold winter's day, there's nothing I enjoy more than playing Christmas music and dancing around the kitchen whilst I'm baking festive treats. And you can create your own special traditions too! Choose a Christmassy recipe from this book, tie on your apron and have fun spending time together!

David

Contents

Christmas cakes and biscuits

Festive showstoppers

Christmas store cupboard

Christmas can be a busy time of year! But if you buy your ingredients in advance and read each recipe carefully, then you can focus on having fun in the kitchen. Here are a few handy tips, tricks and facts to help you.

 Yeast needs the right conditions to start growing. In this book we use dried fast-action yeast. You can use fresh yeast, but you need to double the weight. Always make sure your yeast is in date.

 Nuts are eaten a lot at Christmas time. Nuts are not only tasty; they are also healthy and add a lovely crunchy texture. There are lots of different nuts and it's easy to switch them in a recipe. Try as many different varieties as you can.

 Dried fruits add sweetness to a bake, but they're also full of vitamins, minerals and fibre, which are good for us. Dried fruits are eaten at Christmas time because it's harder to get fresh fruit in the winter.

 Spices are used a lot in Christmas bakes, especially cinnamon, ginger and cloves. If you have lots of different spices in your kitchen cupboard, you can experiment and find your favourite flavour combinations.

 **Food colouring** is a great way to make a plain bake special at Christmas. I recommend using colour gels or pastes as they don't change the consistency of your mixture. Look out for natural food colours that are made from vegetables and fruits. Make sure you have enough red and green as these are the most Christmassy colours.

Root vegetables like carrots, parsnips and sweet potatoes make bread and cakes soft and, most importantly, healthy. Root vegetables are easy to find in winter, so perfect for Christmas recipes.

 Butter and spreads are used in a lot of cakes, pastries and biscuits. Some bakes are known for their buttery flavour, but there are lots of alternatives made with sunflower oil, soy beans or vegetable oil.

 Milks and yogurts were traditionally made with cow's milk. Nowadays, you can buy all kinds of milks and yogurts made from plants, such as oat milk or soya yogurt.

If you have food allergies, or are cooking for someone who does, you need to check the ingredients list carefully.

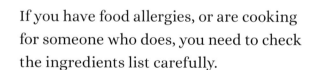

Weighing and measuring

- All recipes are measured in grams (g) and millilitres (ml).

- Tsp = teaspoon. Tbsp = tablespoon.

- The oven temperatures are in degrees Celsius (°C).

- Increase the temperature by 20°C for a non fan-assisted oven.

- Standard cupcake cases are the size in between muffin cases and fairy cake cases.

Great gifts

These gift wrapping ideas add another touch of thoughtfulness to your homemade treats. And, best of all, you can reuse and upcycle leftover everyday items you find in your kitchen.

Make a gift box

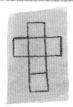

1 Take a large piece of card and draw a cross-shaped template made up of 10cm x 10cm squares. The cross should be 4 squares high and 3 squares wide.

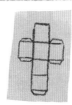

2 Next, add tabs (0.5cm in height) to the top and bottom edges of the side panels and the bottom edge of the bottom panel.

3 Cut around the outside edge, then ask an adult to carefully score along the lines using a ruler and scissors.

4 Draw a fun Christmas design on one side of your template.

5 Turn the template over and fold in all the tabs. Then fold in the panels closest to the side tabs and glue them in place.

6 You should now have a box with a lid that is not stuck down.

7 Place your baked gift or sweets inside the box and close the lid.

Decorative jam jars

Make your special Christmas jam (p. 12) even more special by covering the metal lid with brown paper or leftover Christmas wrapping paper and tightly fastening with string or ribbon. Personalize it by writing and drawing on the top.

Tied sandwich bags

Show off your sweet and spicy popcorn (p. 24) in a clear sandwich bag, perfect for sharing. Scoop in a few handfuls and secure with a bow!

Gift-wrapped tubes

Give your leftover biscuit or crisp container another life! Decorate it with Christmas wrapping paper and fill it with a sweet surprise like the coconut snowballs (p. 14), then add a ribbon or bow.

Equipment list

Before you begin, it's a good idea to check what equipment you might need. Here is a list of the basic equipment you will use in this book, but check each recipe individually too.

Baking paper

Baking tins

Baking trays

Biscuit cutters

Cake tins

Child's safety knife

Cooling rack

Cupcake tray

Digital weighing scales

Festive plates and bowls for serving

Mini foil baking cases

Food processor

Kitchen scissors

Large mixing bowl

Measuring jug

Measuring spoons

Muffin tray (12-hole)

Oven gloves

Oven timer

Pastry brush

Piping bags and nozzles

Rolling pin

Saucepan

Sieve

Spatula

Standard cupcake cases

Hand blender

Tea towel

Whisk

Wooden spoon

Remember to always ask an adult to help when you're baking. And don't forget to wash and dry your hands!

Sweets and edible gifts

Ingredients

700g frozen raspberries
100g caster sugar
1 tsp ground mixed spice
5ml lemon juice
40g chia seeds

Makes 4 jars of jam

Special Christmas jam

This recipe is *really* special because it has raspberries – my favourite fruit for jam – and a touch of mixed spice and lemon to make it even more flavourful. Chia seeds go very sticky when wet, which is perfect for jam. I think the best way to eat it is on porridge, but you'll find lots of recipes in this book where you can use this jam.

Top tip: you can try making this jam with all sorts of fruit, like strawberries, cherries or even blueberries.

Method

1 Add the raspberries, sugar and mixed spice to a small saucepan.

2 Ask an adult to help as you bring the ingredients to a simmer. Let the jam bubble away for 3 minutes, stirring continually to help break down the fruit.

3 Carefully take the pan off the heat, then stir through the lemon juice and chia seeds and leave to cool.

4 When the jam has completely cooled, carefully pour it into 4 jars.

5 Tie some ribbon around the jar and add a little gift label with a festive message on it.

6 Give the jam to a friend as a gift and let them know to keep it in the fridge and use within 2 weeks.

Crunchy peanut butter cups

My husband is called Nik and these nutty treats are his favourite sweets. I make them for his birthday as well as Christmas. Using mini foil baking cases makes them extra special, but you can prepare this recipe in a 20cm x 20cm tin and cut it into squares too.

Ingredients

80g shortbread (or
    digestive biscuits)
60g smooth peanut butter
240g dark chocolate
About 60 roasted peanuts

Makes 20 peanut butter cups

Top tip: you can use almond butter instead of peanut butter and top with almonds.

Method

1 Place 20 mini foil baking cases on a large baking tray. (Or, if using a 20cm x 20cm tin, line the tin with foil to prevent the mixture sticking.)

2 Put the shortbread in a sandwich bag and bash with a rolling pin until crushed into rough breadcrumbs, then tip into a mixing bowl.

3 Break the chocolate into pieces and add to a small microwavable bowl. Ask an adult to help you microwave it for 30 seconds, then stir and repeat until it is melted and smooth.

4 Add the peanut butter to the crushed biscuits and mix until combined. Warm the peanut butter in the microwave for 20 seconds if it is too hard.

5 Put a teaspoonful of melted chocolate into a case, then add a teaspoonful of the biscuit mixture. Top with another teaspoonful of melted chocolate and 3 peanuts.

6 Repeat step 5 until you have used all the mixture. Refrigerate for at least 30 minutes, or until set.

Coconut snowballs

Truffles are fun to make, but it does get a bit messy. I love it because you can lick your hands afterwards and they taste really chocolatey (make sure you wait until the end, though). Adults love truffles, so maybe this is a good present to make for your parents or carers, as long as they like chocolate.

Ingredients

100g dark chocolate
60g soft pitted dates
100ml coconut milk
20g desiccated coconut

Makes 20 truffles

Top tip: roll the truffles in all kinds of coatings like cocoa powder, crushed biscuits, freeze-dried fruit, chopped nuts or even sprinkles.

Method

1 Break the chocolate into pieces and add to a deep bowl, then set aside.

2 Using scissors, cut the dates into chunks, removing any stones, then add the date pieces to a small saucepan.

3 Pour over the coconut milk, then bring to a simmer over a medium heat for 3 minutes.

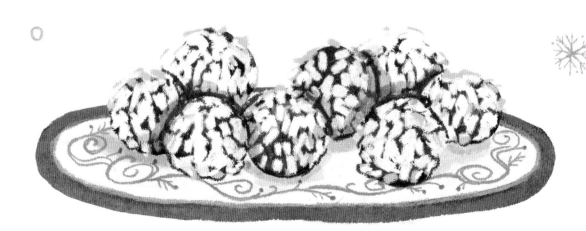

4 Pour the date and coconut milk mixture over the chocolate pieces, leave for 1 minute, then blend with a hand blender until smooth.

5 Cover and chill in the fridge for at least 3 hours.

6 Just before you take the mixture out of the fridge, put the desiccated coconut in a small bowl.

7 This is the messy part! Scoop a small teaspoonful of the truffle mixture into your hands and quickly roll it into a ball shape (you have to be quick to stop the chocolate melting too much).

8 Roll the little ball in the desiccated coconut, then transfer to a plate until you've finished them all.

9 The truffles are best stored in the fridge and eaten within 3 days.

Ingredients

1 lime

150g unsalted butter
(at room temperature)

1 tsp vanilla extract

120g caster sugar

250g plain flour

Green food colour gel

1 medium egg white

180g icing sugar

Makes 30 small
biscuits (or 20
larger biscuits)

Shortbread trees

Shortbread is a buttery, crumbly biscuit that is perfect for giving as a present as it tastes delicious and keeps nicely. For this recipe, we use royal icing, which sets really hard and gives the biscuits an extra crunch. You will need a small tree-shaped cutter, but if you don't have one, just use a different-shaped cutter, like a star or a circle shape for a bauble, and decorate with different coloured icing.

Method

1 Line 2 large baking trays with baking paper.

2 Ask an adult to help you carefully zest the lime using a fine grater into a large mixing bowl.

3 Beat together the butter, vanilla extract and 100g of the caster sugar, then beat until creamy and smooth.

4 Add the flour, then use your hands to mix everything together until it forms a stiff dough (if crumbly, add a little water).

5 On a lightly floured surface, roll out the dough until it is 1cm thick.

6 Cut out the dough with your tree-shaped cutter and place the trees on the baking trays.

7 Once you've used all the dough, chill the trays in the fridge for 30 minutes.

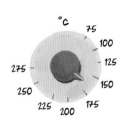

8 Preheat oven to 170°C (fan-assisted).

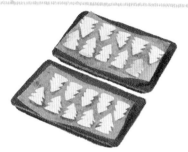

9 Take the trays out of the fridge, then bake for 12–15 minutes until golden brown at the edges.

10 For the topping, add the remaining 20g of caster sugar and the green food colouring to a sandwich bag and shake them so that the sugar turns green.

11 Mix together the egg white and icing sugar until you have a smooth, runny icing.

12 Once the biscuits are baked and cooled, dip them face down into the icing, then sprinkle with the green sugar. It takes a few hours for royal icing to set really hard.

Top tip: add orange, lemon or grapefruit zest if you like your shortbread extra zesty!

Ingredients

12 flaked almonds

12 currants

6 dried cranberries

6 mini pretzels

400g dark chocolate

100g white chocolate

Makes 1 slab of bark

Reindeer chocolate bark

Who wouldn't like a big slab of chocolate as a gift? Here we use nuts, dried fruit and pretzels to make reindeer faces that are set into the chocolate. The reindeer design is especially Christmassy, but you can sprinkle over any toppings you like. Just remember to use something crunchy for an interesting texture.

Top tip: make smaller slabs of chocolate bark if you want to gift them to a few people!

Method

1 Prepare the toppings first. Put the flaked almonds, currants and cranberries in separate little bowls.

2 Break the pretzels in half (or ask an adult to cut them carefully with a knife) and add to another little bowl.

3 Line a large baking tray with baking paper.

4 Break the dark chocolate into a microwavable bowl. Ask an adult to help you microwave it for 30 seconds, then stir and repeat until the chocolate is melted and smooth.

5 Ask an adult to pour the dark chocolate onto the baking paper.

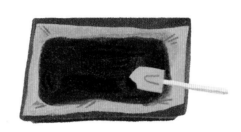

6 Use a spatula to spread it around until you have a rectangular-shaped slab of chocolate that is about the size of an A4 piece of paper.

7 Repeat step 4 with the white chocolate and leave to cool a little.

8 Drop 6 teaspoonfuls of white chocolate onto the dark chocolate slab (these will be the reindeer heads).

9 Add the pretzels for antlers, flaked almonds for ears, currants for eyes and a cranberry for the nose.

10 Chill the baking tray in the fridge and allow to set (this may take up to 1 hour).

11 Once the chocolate has set, you can either give the whole slab as a present, or you can break it into individual pieces.

12 If you are gifting this as a big slab, I suggest wrapping it in baking paper and tying it with a ribbon. If you've broken it into pieces, use clear sandwich bags.

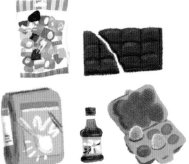

Melting meringue snowpeople

Meringues are sweet and crunchy and chewy in the middle. For this recipe, your piping skills will be put to the test as we pipe meringue and then pipe chocolate on top. Decorate the snowpeople with chocolate and sweets or, for a healthier option, use nuts, seeds and dried fruit. You will need 2 piping bags for this recipe, but if you don't have any, then sandwich bags work just as well. Store the finished meringues in an airtight container to stop them going soft.

Ingredients

2 medium egg whites

100g caster sugar

½ tsp vanilla extract

50g milk chocolate

54 dolly mixture sweets
(or other little sweets
or nuts, seeds and
dried fruit)

Makes 18 meringues

Method

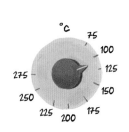

1 Preheat oven to 110°C (fan-assisted).

2 Line 2 large baking trays with baking paper.

3 Crack the eggs, 1 at a time, over a little bowl and let the egg white drip through your fingers, while containing the yolk in your open hand.

4 Use an electric mixer to beat the egg whites until stiff and fluffy (this may take 3–5 minutes).

5 While still whisking, add 1 teaspoonful of caster sugar and count to 10. Repeat until you have used up the sugar. Then add the vanilla and whisk for another 30 seconds.

6 Rub a little of the mixture between your finger and thumb. It should be smooth, without any sugar granules.

7 Ask an adult to hold open your piping bag, then spoon the meringue mixture inside. Bring the top of the bag together and twist.

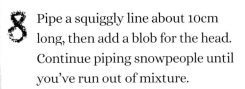

8 Pipe a squiggly line about 10cm long, then add a blob for the head. Continue piping snowpeople until you've run out of mixture.

9 Bake for 1 hour, then switch off the oven and leave the snowpeople inside the oven for another hour.

10 Break the chocolate into a microwavable bowl. Ask an adult to help you microwave it for 30 seconds, then stir and repeat until it is melted and smooth.

11 Ask an adult to pour the melted chocolate carefully into a smaller piping bag. If using a sandwich bag, snip a small opening at the tip (about 1mm).

12 Pipe on the eyes, mouth and 3 blobs for buttons. Add a sweet to each blob. Allow the chocolate to set before eating or gifting.

Top tip: give your snowpeople some personality! You can use marshmallows and fruit leather to make hats and scarves.

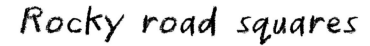

Rocky road squares

Are you ready to rocky-road around the Christmas tree? Then this recipe is for you! Rocky road can be made with white, milk or dark chocolate. If you make it with white chocolate, it reminds me of snow, especially because it has a nice crunch, just like snow. I've suggested using digestive biscuits here, but you can use any biscuits you like. Maybe you have some left over from other recipes in this book?

Ingredients

200g digestive biscuits
50g unsalted peanuts
70g dried cranberries
150g mini marshmallows
400g white chocolate
2 tsp custard powder
80g plain yogurt
Christmas sprinkles

Makes 16 bite-sized pieces

Method

1 Line a 20cm x 20cm tin with baking paper.

2 Put the biscuits in a sandwich bag. Bash gently with a rolling pin until crushed, then add to a mixing bowl.

3 Add most of the peanuts and cranberries (save about ¼ to sprinkle on top), then add the marshmallows and mix everything together with a wooden spoon.

4 Break the chocolate into pieces and add to a microwavable bowl. Ask an adult to help you microwave it for 30 seconds, then stir and repeat until it is melted and smooth.

5 Leave the chocolate to cool a little.

6 Add the custard powder and yogurt to another small bowl and stir until combined.

7 Pour the yogurt mixture into the white chocolate and stir until smooth. Add this to the mixing bowl and stir until everything is coated.

8 Transfer to the tin and gently press down so that the mixture fills the corners of the tin and is roughly level.

9 Top with the leftover peanuts and cranberries, then add your Christmas sprinkles.

10 Chill the rocky road for at least 2 hours in the fridge.

11 Once the rocky road has set, ask an adult to help you cut it into 4 rows and then each row into 4 squares so that you have 16 pieces.

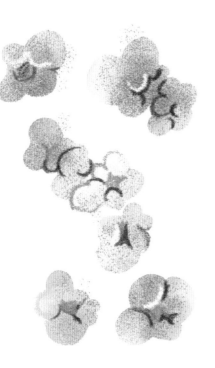

Sweet and spicy popcorn

I love popcorn and eat it all year round. I like it sweet, but my husband likes it salty. This version is perfect for both of us as it is a little sweet, a little salty, and the dusting of cinnamon gives it a special Christmas twist!

Top tip: package the popcorn in clear piping bags, tie the tops with ribbon and then you have perfect gift bags!

Ingredients

1 tsp brown sugar

¼ tsp salt

½ tsp cocoa powder

½ tsp ground cinnamon

60g popcorn kernels

1 tbsp vegetable oil

20g butter

Makes 4–6 portions

Method

1 Mix the sugar, salt, cocoa powder and cinnamon together in a small bowl, then set aside.

2 Ask an adult to help you with popping the popcorn kernels. First, measure out the popcorn kernels into a large mixing bowl.

3 Add the oil to a medium saucepan (that has a lid) and heat on a medium setting, keeping the lid off as the oil heats up.

4 Carefully add 2 kernels to the pan.

5 When 1 of the kernels pops, add the butter, the rest of the kernels and then the saucepan lid.

6 As the popcorn pops, ask an adult to shake the pan once or twice.

7 Once there are gaps of more than 2 seconds between pops, remove from the heat and tip the kernels into your large mixing bowl.

8 Sprinkle over the sugar, salt and spice mix and quickly toss together with a wooden spoon.

9 Allow to cool before popping the popcorn in your mouth.

Ingredients

180g ground almonds
130g icing sugar
30ml water
½ tsp almond extract
Red food colour gel
Green food colour gel

Makes 30 pieces

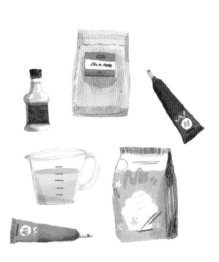

Marzipan holly

Marzipan is my favourite thing about Christmas. I just love it SO much!!! Marzipan is like nutty, edible Play-Doh, and you can use it to create whatever shapes you want. My twin brother once made me a gift of marzipan vegetables for Christmas because he only had green food colouring!

Method

1 Put the ground almonds and icing sugar in a food processor and pulse twice until combined.

2 Add the water and almond extract and pulse until the mixture looks like breadcrumbs. (If you don't have a food processor, you can rub and squish it with your hands.)

3 Tip out onto a clean surface, then squash it all together and knead until it becomes a smooth dough.

4 Take a golf-ball sized piece of marzipan, add a small blob of red food colouring, then squish and squash the dough until it turns red.

5 Add a blob of green food colouring to the rest of the marzipan and squish and squash it until it all turns green.

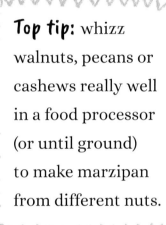

Top tip: whizz walnuts, pecans or cashews really well in a food processor (or until ground) to make marzipan from different nuts.

6 Roll out the green marzipan until it is about 0.5cm thick and cut out shapes with a holly leaf cutter. Use a dusting of icing sugar if it is sticking to the surface.

7 Pinch off little pieces of red marzipan and roll into berries.

8 Dip your finger in water and dab the end of each holly leaf, squashing it slightly. Wait for a minute then gently press 2 berries onto the end of each leaf.

Marzipan Christmas creations

If you have more food colourings and decorations, try making some different marzipan creations to share with your friends and family.

Christmas crowns

Add a pinch of turmeric to colour the marzipan a golden yellow, then use a crown biscuit cutter to cut out shapes (or use a little knife to cut round a template). Decorate the crowns with nuts, seeds, dried fruit, sweets or any of your favourite toppings.

Snowy trees

Roll green marzipan pieces into cones, snip around the sides with scissors to make branches, then dust with icing sugar to make them look snowy.

Marzipan potatoes

In Germany, they eat marzipan potatoes at Christmas, which are my favourite. It's fun to make potatoes and really easy. You just roll balls of marzipan, make them a little uneven with your fingers, then dust them with cocoa powder and roll in your hands again.

Marzipan fruits

If you're feeling creative, have a go at making traditional marzipan fruits. Use different food colourings when preparing the marzipan and see how realistic you can make your fruit.

Party food

Ingredients

Dough:

400g strong white bread flour (plus extra for dusting)

100g strong wholemeal bread flour

7g fast-action yeast (1 sachet)

1 tsp salt

300ml warm water

Sauce:

1 tin of chopped tomatoes

1 tsp dried oregano

½ tsp salt

Toppings:

100g Cheddar cheese

100g Red Leicester cheese

1 red pepper

1 green pepper

8 green olives

50g tinned sweetcorn (drained)

Makes 6 mini pizzas

Christmas jumper pizzas

Everyone loves a bright and funny Christmas jumper, and with this recipe you get to design your own AND eat it! Making pizzas is always a fun bake, and here people can use their favourite toppings and let their imaginations run wild.

Method

1 In a large mixing bowl, combine the flours, yeast, salt and water until a sticky dough forms, then allow to rest for 5 minutes.

2 Tip the dough out onto a lightly floured surface and knead for 3 minutes (do not use any extra flour; it doesn't matter if it starts off sticky).

3 Return the dough to the bowl, cover and allow to rise in a warm place until it doubles in size (this will take over 1 hour).

4 While the dough is rising, tip the chopped tomatoes into a small saucepan with the oregano and salt. Simmer gently for 15 minutes, then leave to cool.

5 Line 2 large baking trays with baking paper.

6 Preheat oven to 200°C (fan-assisted).

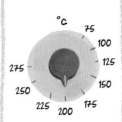

7 On a lightly floured surface, roll out the dough until you have a rectangular shape that is about 50cm x 40cm.

8 Using a pizza cutter, slice in half widthways, then cut each half into 3 pieces.

9 Cut each of those pieces into 1 big piece and 2 smaller pieces (to make the jumper body and the sleeves).

10 Lay a big piece (for the jumper body) onto the baking paper, then press the 2 smaller pieces (for the sleeves) onto the top corners of the jumper.

11 Cut off 1cm from the end of each sleeve and press these pieces onto the top of the jumper to form a neck.

12 Repeat steps 10–11 to make the rest of your pizza jumpers, then spread with the tomato base, sprinkle on the cheese and decorate with the rest of the toppings.

13 Bake for 15 minutes, then allow to cool for 10 minutes before serving.

Top tip: make regular round pizzas and decorate them like baubles!

Festive dips

Red and green are the most Christmassy colours EVER. As there are loads of red and green vegetables, this means making Christmas dips is easy! The whizzed-up cannellini beans make the dips super smooth and all the more delicious. Serve your dips with some carrot or cucumber batons or even some star cheese crackers (see the opposite page).

Ingredients

Red dip:

100g of roasted red
  peppers from a jar
  (drained)
120g of cannellini beans
  (drained)
1 garlic clove (minced)
30g walnuts
A pinch of salt
1 tsp ground cumin

Green dip:

1 ripe avocado
120g cannellini beans
  (drained)
A pinch of salt
20g fresh basil
1 garlic clove (minced)

Makes 2 big bowls of dip

Method

1 For the red dip, add the red peppers and cannellini beans to a food processor, then whizz together. If you want the dip to be very smooth, keep whizzing for another 2 minutes. (Use the remaining beans for your green dip.)

2 Add the garlic, walnuts, salt and cumin, then whizz everything together until combined. Scoop the dip into a small bowl, ready to serve. Ask an adult to help you clean the food processor before you make the green dip.

3 For the green dip, ask an adult to help you slice the avocado in half, remove the stone and scoop out the flesh with a spoon.

4 Add the avocado, cannellini beans, salt, basil and garlic to the food processor and whizz until smooth.

5 Serve with vegetable batons, breadsticks or crackers, and enjoy!

Ingredients

80g plain flour (plus extra
    for dusting)
20g wholemeal plain flour
½ tsp baking powder
30g butter
50g Cheddar cheese (grated)
1 tsp Marmite (or Vegemite)
2 tsp water

Makes 20 crackers

Star cheese crackers

Most families buy lots of cheese at Christmas time. I LOVE Cheddar, but you can make these biscuits with any leftover cheese you have around. Some people love Marmite and some people hate it. For these biscuits, Marmite isn't the main flavour, so hopefully everyone will like them. It's a super-simple recipe and if you don't have a food processor, you can rub the ingredients together with your fingers instead.

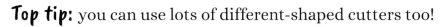

Top tip: you can use lots of different-shaped cutters too!

Method

1 Line 2 large baking trays with baking paper.

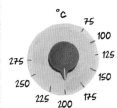

2 Preheat oven to 200ºC (fan-assisted).

3 Add the flours, baking powder and butter to a food processor and pulse until it looks like breadcrumbs.

4 Next, add the grated cheese, Marmite and water, and pulse until combined.

5 Tip out onto a clean, lightly floured surface and bring together to form a dough.

6 Roll out the dough until it is about 0.5cm thick. Then cut out with a 6cm star-shaped biscuit cutter.

7 Place on the baking trays and prick each star 4 times with a fork.

8 Bake for 10 minutes, then leave to cool on a cooling rack.

Christmas tree pull-apart bread

You may have heard of "tear and share" bread – a big bread that is easy to pull apart into smaller pieces. This version is perfect for a party and goes well with the festive dips (p. 32).

Ingredients

25g spinach

25g fresh basil

220ml warm water

400g strong white bread flour (plus extra for dusting)

7g fast-action yeast (1 sachet)

1 tsp salt

40g Cheddar cheese (grated)

2 tsp semi-skimmed milk

1 tsp maple syrup (or runny honey)

1 tbsp poppy seeds

1 tbsp sesame seeds

Makes 8–10 servings

Method

1 Line a large baking tray with baking paper.

2 Put the spinach, basil and water in a blender and blitz until you have green water.

3 Put the flour, yeast and salt in a mixing bowl, then add the green water and mix together to make a rough dough.

4 Cover and leave for 3 minutes.

5 Tip the dough out onto a lightly floured surface and knead for 5 minutes (do not use any extra flour; it doesn't matter if it starts off sticky).

6 Return the dough to the bowl, cover and leave in a warm place until it doubles in size (this will take at least 1 hour).

7 On a lightly floured surface, roll out the dough to a rectangle shape that is about 35cm x 25cm.

8 Cut away each side of the dough at an angle so that you have 1 large triangle and 2 smaller triangles.

9 Take the 2 offcuts and flip them onto the baking tray to make another large triangle shape.

10 Sprinkle over the grated cheese, then place the remaining triangle on top.

11 Ask an adult to help you cut 8 tabs into each side, using kitchen scissors.

12 Gently lift each tab and twist it round and round a few times, then place back down.

13 Cover and leave your tree dough to rise until it doubles in size.

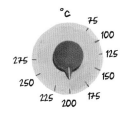

14 Preheat oven to 200°C (fan-assisted).

15 Mix together the milk and maple syrup in a bowl, then brush over the tree. Sprinkle over the seeds and bake for 15 minutes, then allow to cool.

Ingredients

300g King Edward potatoes
(once peeled)

100g of tinned sweetcorn
(drained)

½ tsp salt

200g filo pastry

30g butter

12 tsp cranberry sauce

Makes 20 parcels

Method

Filo pastry presents

Lots of people like to give presents to each other at Christmas, and here are some tasty filo pastry presents for your Christmas party. You can make the presents personal by adding different sauce fillings for different people – I love mustard! These are best eaten warm while they're still crunchy.

1 Peel then chop the potatoes into 1cm cubes and add to a small saucepan with enough water to cover them.

2 Ask an adult to help you bring the water to a boil. Simmer for 10 minutes until the potato cubes are soft, then drain.

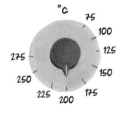

3 Preheat oven to 200°C (fan-assisted).

4 Line a large baking tray with baking paper.

5 In a bowl, toss together the potato cubes, sweetcorn and salt, then set aside.

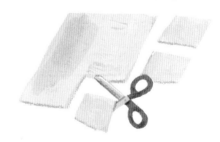

6 Prepare the filo pastry by cutting it into squares that are about 15cm x 15cm. You need 60 squares in total (3 layers of filo per parcel).

7 Add the butter to a small microwavable bowl and ask an adult to melt it in the microwave (about 5–10 seconds).

8 To make the parcels, place a square of pastry on a chopping board and brush all over with a little melted butter (if you don't have a brush, use your fingers).

9 Add another layer of pastry, brush with butter again, then add a final layer and brush with butter.

10 Take a spoonful of filling and place in the centre of the square, then add a teaspoonful of cranberry sauce on top.

11 Gather all the sides and scrunch together at the top.

12 Transfer to the baking tray, then repeat steps 8–11 to make the rest of your parcels.

13 Bake for 20 minutes until golden and crispy, then leave to cool on a cooling rack.

Ingredients

400g King Edward
  potatoes (once peeled)
200g parsnips (once peeled)
½ tsp salt
50g plain flour
2 medium eggs
80g panko breadcrumbs
1 tsp paprika
1 tbsp vegetable oil
70g Cheddar cheese

Makes 14 croquettes

Cheesy Christmas croquettes

Roast potatoes are often the yummiest part of a Christmas dinner, but that's because people haven't tried these cheesy Christmas croquettes yet! They are crunchy on the outside, then SO soft and creamy in the middle. You can eat them as part of a dinner, as a festive snack on their own, or simply dip them into your favourite sauce and enjoy!

Method

1 Peel the potatoes and parsnips and chop into 1cm pieces.

2 Add to a saucepan with enough water to cover them. Add the salt and bring to a simmer, cooking for 10–12 minutes.

3 Ask an adult to help you drain the water. Mash until smooth, then set aside to cool.

4 Line a large baking tray with baking paper.

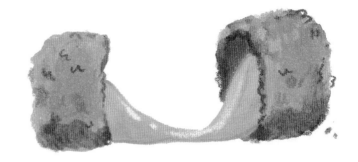

5 Ask an adult to help you cut the Cheddar into 14 cubes.

6 Put the flour in a small bowl. Crack the egg into another bowl and whisk with a fork.

7 Toss together the panko breadcrumbs, paprika and oil in another little bowl.

8 Take a big spoonful of the mashed potato and parsnip and squash it into a disc in your hand.

9 Add a cube of cheese to the middle and shape the potato and parsnip around the cheese.

10 Once all 14 are finished, pop them in the fridge for 10 minutes.

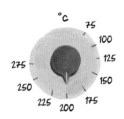

11 Preheat oven to 200°C (fan-assisted).

12 Take your croquettes out of the fridge. One by one, roll them in the flour, then in the egg, then finally in the breadcrumbs. Transfer to the baking tray.

13 Once all the croquettes are ready, bake for 12–14 minutes until nicely golden.

14 Allow to cool a bit before eating; otherwise the cheese will be too hot.

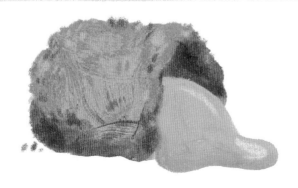

Sweet and sticky sausage rolls

I don't eat meat, so I use veggie sausages for this recipe, but you can use whatever sausages you like. The dough here needs lots of resting time in the fridge, which is the perfect moment for you to wrap your presents or decorate your Christmas tree.

Ingredients

150g strong white bread flour (plus extra for dusting)

150g plain flour

½ tsp baking powder

200g cold unsalted butter (diced into 1cm cubes)

140ml cold water

12 chipolatas or small sausages (uncooked)

½ jar of cranberry sauce

20ml semi-skimmed milk

Makes 24 pastries

Method

1 Put the flours, baking powder and cubes of butter in a mixing bowl and toss together.

2 Pour in the cold water, lightly mix with a spatula, then gently knead to a dough (try not to squash the butter too much; you should still be able to see whole bits of butter).

3 On a lightly floured surface, roll out the dough until it is 1cm thick, then fold in half, wrap in cling film and chill in the fridge for 30 minutes.

4 While the dough is chilling, ask an adult to help slice the sausages in half lengthways and set aside (remember to wash your hands after).

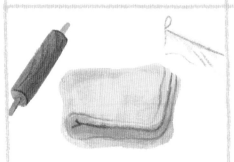

5 Repeat step 3 one more time.

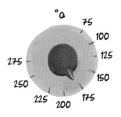

6 Preheat oven to 180°C (fan-assisted).

Top tip: if you prefer, you can use tomato ketchup, barbecue or spicy sauce instead of the cranberry sauce.

7 Line 2 large baking trays with baking paper.

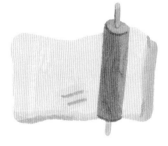

8 On a lightly floured surface, roll out the pastry to make a rectangle shape, about 40cm x 24cm.

9 Spread with the cranberry sauce, then ask an adult to help you cut the pastry widthways into 24 equal pieces.

10 With the sauce on the inside, wrap a pastry strip around a sausage half, then place on the baking tray.

11 Repeat step 10 to make all 24 wrapped sausages, then brush them all with the milk.

12 Bake for 25 minutes until nice and golden, then leave to cool on a cooling rack.

Ingredients

Pastry:

80g butter (plus extra for
    greasing)
140g plain flour
20g plain wholemeal flour
50g icing sugar
1 tsp ground cinnamon
35ml semi-skimmed milk

Filling:

160g strawberry jam (or
    special Christmas jam)
40g flaked almonds
20g dried cranberries
40g raisins
1 tbsp icing sugar (for
    dusting)

Makes 12 pies

Fruity "mince" pies

When you smell a mince pie, you know it's Christmas. These mince pies are especially for kids as they are fruity like a Christmas jam tart. They fill the kitchen with lovely smells when they are baking because of the cinnamon in the pastry. I used circular and star-shaped cutters for this recipe, but you can try out all kinds of shapes to top the pies.

Method

1 Add the butter, flours, icing sugar and cinnamon to a food processor and whizz until you have breadcrumbs. Add the milk and whizz again. (If you don't have a food processor, simply rub the butter into the dry ingredients, then stir in the milk with a blunt knife.)

2 Tip out onto a clean surface and bring together with your hands, squashing it until you have a dough.

3 Wrap and chill in the fridge for 30 minutes.

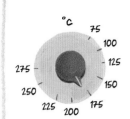

4 Preheat oven to 180°C (fan-assisted).

5 To make the filling, mix together the jam, almonds, cranberries and raisins.

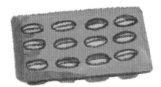

6 Grease a 12-hole cupcake tray with butter, then take the pastry out of the fridge and roll it out on a lightly floured surface until it is 0.5cm thick.

7 Use a 9cm biscuit cutter to cut 12 discs out of the pastry.

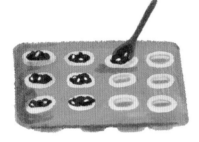

8 Press each pastry disc into a hole in the tin and add a big spoonful of the filling to each pastry case.

9 Bring all the offcuts of pastry together and roll out again.

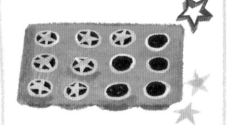

10 Use a star-shaped cutter to cut out 12 stars, then place a star on top of each pie.

11 Bake for 25 minutes, then leave to cool on a cooling rack. Dust with icing sugar before serving.

Orange trifles

My grandma always makes trifle for Christmas. I love trifle, but I don't like the soggy cake. This recipe has all my favourite elements – jelly, fruit, custard and a creamy yogurt on top – but leaves out the soggy cake. All the layers look so pretty, making these a brilliant dessert for a party.

Top tip: try adding chopped strawberries with strawberry jelly, or raspberries with raspberry jelly. Yum!

Ingredients

4 clementines
135g orange jelly cubes
35g custard powder
25g caster sugar
500ml semi-skimmed milk
200g Greek yogurt
Christmas sprinkles

Makes 8 small trifles

Method

1 Ask an adult to help you zest 2 of the clementines and set the zest aside.

2 Peel all the clementines and share out the pieces between the glasses (you can have 1 or 2 pieces yourself if you'd like a snack).

3 Tear the jelly into cubes and add to a measuring jug. Ask an adult to help you pour over 200ml of boiling water, then stir with a fork until all the jelly pieces have dissolved.

4 Add 500ml cold water, stir, then divide the jelly liquid equally between the glasses.

5 Chill in the fridge for at least 2 hours until the jelly is set.

6 To make the custard, add the custard powder, sugar and clementine zest to a small saucepan.

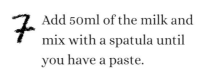

7 Add 50ml of the milk and mix with a spatula until you have a paste.

8 Add the rest of the milk and, with the help of an adult, heat over a medium heat, stirring all the time until thickened (this will take about 1 minute, so keep stirring)!

9 Allow the custard to cool down slightly, then pour it into the glasses and return to the fridge to chill for at least 1 hour.

10 Add the Greek yogurt to a mixing bowl, and give it a stir. Spoon the yogurt into the glasses.

11 Top the trifles with some sprinkles, then serve.

Christmas slushy

There are a lot of adult drinks at Christmas like wine, eggnog and sherry, so here is a colourful fruity drink just for kids! Cranberries and oranges are Christmas fruits, which is good because they're also colourful enough for a party. Can you think of other fun drink ideas for Christmas?

Ingredients

400ml orange juice
500ml cranberry juice
Spiced Christmas cordial

Makes 6 servings

Method

1 Ask an adult to help you pour the orange juice into a small jug.

2 Pour the juice into 2 ice cube trays.

3 Freeze for at least 3 hours.

4 Pour the cranberry juice into 6 small glasses.

5 Add the orange ice cubes to a food processor or blender and blitz for 10–30 seconds or until they go slushy.

6 Spoon the slush into the glasses and top with a drizzle of cordial.

Christmas cakes
and biscuits

Ingredients

Cupcakes:

130g caster sugar

100ml vegetable oil

2 medium eggs

1 tsp vanilla extract

100g King Edward
    potatoes (once peeled)

120g plain flour

1½ tsp baking powder

40g raisins

Decoration:

30g unsalted butter (at
    room temperature)

150g icing sugar

1 tsp vanilla extract

2 tsp boiling water

100g white chocolate
    buttons

20 raisins

Makes 12 cupcakes

Snowy owl cupcakes

Owls are so cute, so who wouldn't want an owl cupcake? Snowy owls are all white and live in snowy areas of the world. They are hard to see because they are camouflaged in the snow. These cupcakes can't hide as easily – they're so delicious everyone will seek them out.

Method

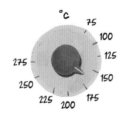

1 Preheat oven to 160°C (fan-assisted).

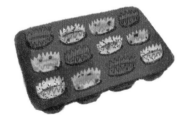

2 Prepare a 12-hole muffin tray with cupcake cases.

3 Beat together the sugar, oil, eggs and vanilla.

4 Peel the potatoes, then finely grate into the mixture and stir together.

5 Fold in the flour and baking powder until combined, then add the raisins and do a final mix.

6 Divide the mixture equally between the paper cases (about ¾ full) and bake for 18 minutes.

7 Allow to cool fully before decorating.

8 Mix together the butter, icing sugar and vanilla (it will look very crumbly, but don't worry).

9 Beat in a teaspoonful of boiling water. Keep adding teaspoonfuls of boiling water until you have a thick icing.

10 Spread a thin layer of icing onto each cupcake.

11 Carefully cut some chocolate buttons in half, then layer them over the bottom half of the icing to make the feathers.

12 Add whole chocolate buttons for the eyes and pieces for the ears. Using a little of the leftover icing, stick raisins in place for a beak and pupils.

Top tip: add 2 teaspoonfuls of cocoa powder to the icing and use milk chocolate buttons to make tawny owls.

Red velvet Santa hats

These cakes are quick and easy to make and taste delicious! Red velvet cake is actually a chocolate cake, but you don't use a lot of cocoa powder, so the cake doesn't come out brown. It is up to you how much red food colouring you put into the cake. The yogurt in this cake helps the cake rise and makes it really soft.

Ingredients

Cakes:

75ml vegetable oil (plus extra for greasing)

140g caster sugar

100g live natural yogurt

1 tsp vanilla extract

Red food colour gel

1 medium egg

125g plain flour

1 tsp cocoa powder

½ tsp baking powder

½ tsp bicarbonate of soda

Decoration:

50g icing sugar

50g mini white marshmallows

Makes 8 cakes

Method

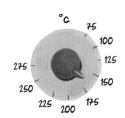

1 Preheat oven to 160°C (fan-assisted).

2 Grease the inside of a 20cm round tin with a little oil, making sure you cover all of the tin.

3 In a large mixing bowl, beat together the oil, sugar, yogurt, vanilla and red food colouring.

4 Crack the egg over the bowl and beat into the mixture.

5 In a separate bowl, toss together the flour, cocoa powder, baking powder and bicarbonate of soda.

6 Tip the dry ingredients into the wet mixture and stir until combined.

7 Pour into the tin and bake for 25–30 minutes (or until a skewer comes out clean).

8 Ask an adult to take the tin out of the oven, then leave the cake to cool on a cooling rack before removing it from the tin.

9 Slice the cake in half, then in half again and again until you have 8 slices.

10 Tip the icing sugar into the bowl, then add 2 teaspoonfuls of water and mix.

11 Mix together and keep adding a teaspoonful of water until your icing becomes thick and sticky.

12 Cut the marshmallows into small pieces (about 0.5cm big) on a chopping board, then add to the icing.

13 Spoon the marshmallow icing onto the rims and tops of the cake slices so that they look like Santa hats!

Ingredients

Cake:

130g caster sugar

130g soft brown sugar

200ml vegetable oil

4 medium eggs

220g carrots (once peeled)

250g plain flour

3 tsp baking powder

1 tsp ground cinnamon

Decoration:

120g icing sugar

½ tsp almond extract

20ml water

Christmas sprinkles

4 strawberry laces

Makes 12 servings

Cracker carrot cake

I LOVE carrot cake, but you can also use parsnip, sweet potato or butternut squash instead in this recipe. Did you know that root vegetables were popular ingredients in baking when we didn't have a lot of sugar or butter? They make cakes soft and sweet as well as a little bit healthier, so everyone's happy!

Method

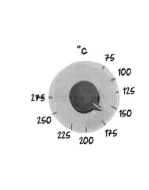

1 Preheat oven to 160°C (fan-assisted).

2 Grease and line two 20cm loaf tins with baking paper.

3 In a large mixing bowl, beat together the sugars and oil until smooth. Crack the eggs, one at a time, over the bowl, then beat into the mixture.

4 Ask an adult to help you peel and finely grate the carrots. Add to the bowl and mix through the batter.

5 Add the flour, baking powder and cinnamon and stir until just combined.

6 Divide the mixture between the 2 tins and bake for 30–40 minutes (or until a skewer comes out clean). For the first 20 minutes, try not to open the oven to prevent the cakes collapsing.

7 Allow to cool completely, then turn the cakes out of the tins and peel off the baking paper.

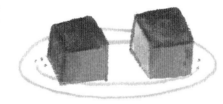

8 Turn each cake upside down. Place 1 in the middle of a plate, then cut the other in half so that you have 2 square pieces (10cm x 10cm).

9 Remove triangles of cake from 1 side of each cake half, then place each half at either end of the second cake.

10 Beat together the icing sugar, almond extract and water until you have a thick icing.

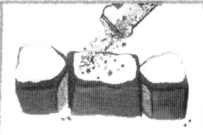

11 Spread the icing onto the cake and add your sprinkles.

12 Stick the strawberry laces at each end to make ribbons.

Ingredients

150g golden syrup

100g soft pitted dates

80g unsalted butter (plus extra for greasing)

70g soft brown sugar

2 medium eggs

1 tsp vanilla extract

150g plain flour

1 tsp baking powder

4 tsp semi-skimmed milk

Makes 6 puddings

Steamed syrup puddings

Steamed syrup pudding is a bit of an old-fashioned recipe, and I remember my mum making it when we were kids. This version is easier because you prepare it in mugs and then zap it in the microwave, but it still tastes delicious! These easy, speedy puddings are best eaten fresh with a little cream or ice cream.

Method

1 Grease 6 microwavable mugs with a little butter, then divide the syrup equally between the mugs.

2 Add the dates, butter and sugar to a food processor and blitz until smooth.

3 Crack the eggs into the food processor, add the vanilla and blitz again until combined.

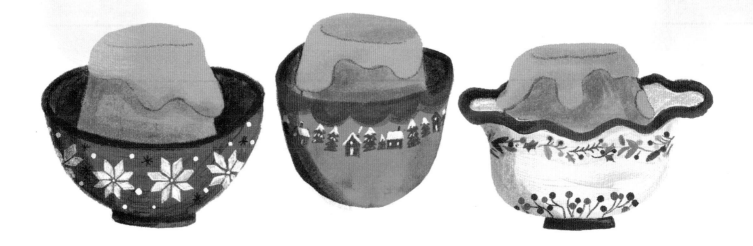

4 In a mixing bowl, toss together the flour and baking powder.

5 Spoon the mixture from the food processor into the mixing bowl, add the milk, then stir until combined.

6 Divide equally between the mugs (don't worry if it doesn't look like much batter; it rises a lot when cooked).

7 Microwave 2 puddings for 4 minutes on full power.

8 Ask an adult to help you take them out of the microwave, then leave them to sit for 4 minutes.

9 Once the puddings have cooled, ask an adult to turn the puddings out into bowls (be careful as the syrup is hot).

10 Repeat steps 7–9 with the rest of the mugs until you have 6 puddings.

11 Serve with custard, yogurt or ice cream.

Top tip: try adding ground spices or citrus zest to the batter for extra Christmassy flavour!

Mini chocolate logs

Bûche de Noël, or Yule log, is a traditional chocolate Christmas cake originally from France, but which is now baked at Christmas time in lots of countries. It's a light, decadent cake that is filled with buttercream and rolled up to make a log shape. Don't worry if your sponge cracks a little as you wrap it up. The cake will still taste delicious and be VERY chocolatey, which is the most important thing.

Ingredients

Cakes:

3 medium eggs

100g caster sugar

80g plain flour

20g cocoa powder

½ tsp baking powder

30g butter (plus extra for greasing)

Decoration:

70g icing sugar

1 tsp vanilla extract

200g dark chocolate

A little hot water (boiled)

Makes 8 logs

Method

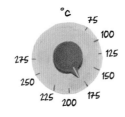

1 Preheat oven to 180°C (fan-assisted).

2 Grease the inside of a 33cm x 25cm Swiss roll tin with butter and line it with baking paper.

3 Crack the eggs into a large mixing bowl, then add the sugar. Use an electric whisk to beat them together until you have a thick mixture that leaves a trail like a ribbon.

4 Toss together the flour, cocoa powder and baking powder in another bowl, then add to the egg mixture, a bit at a time, gently folding it in with a spatula to keep it light and airy.

5 Pour the mixture carefully into the tin and use a spatula to spread it out, then bake for 15 minutes.

6 Allow to cool for 2 minutes, then turn out onto a cooling rack, keeping the baking paper in place.

7 While the cake is still warm, roll up 1 short side until you reach the middle. Then roll the other side to the middle, wrap in a tea towel and leave to cool.

8 To make the buttercream, rub the butter and icing sugar together until you have a crumbly mixture. Add the vanilla and 1 teaspoonful of hot water, then beat until smooth (add another teaspoonful of hot water if you need to).

9 Unwrap your cake and cut down the middle so you have 2 rolls.

10 Unroll each cake and remove the baking paper. Spread each cake with a thin layer of buttercream, then roll up again tightly, using your tea towel.

11 Slice each roll into 4 so that you have 8 mini rolls.

12 Ask an adult to help you microwave the chocolate for 30 seconds, then stir and repeat until it is melted and smooth.

13 Allow the chocolate to cool down a little, then spoon it over the rolls and spread it around. Use a fork to make marks along the rolls so that they look like little logs.

14 Allow the chocolate logs to set in the fridge for at least 10 minutes, then serve.

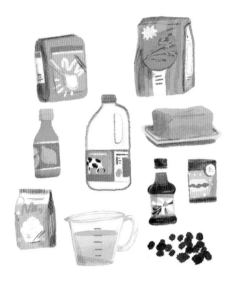

Snowpeople scones

Not everyone gets snow at Christmas time, but everyone can build a scone snowperson. The recipe here gives you the basic decoration, but you can use sweets, seeds, nuts, fruits or whatever you can think of to add more personality to your snowpeople.

Ingredients

Scones:

350g plain flour (plus extra for dusting)

2 tsp baking powder

50g caster sugar

80g unsalted butter

170ml semi-skimmed milk

1 tsp vanilla extract

1 tsp lemon juice

Decoration:

140g icing sugar

20ml water

1 tsp vanilla extract

A handful of currants

Makes 8 scones

Method

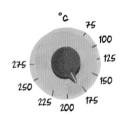

1 Preheat oven to 180°C (fan-assisted).

2 Line a large baking tray with baking paper.

3 In a mixing bowl, rub the flour, baking powder, sugar and butter together with your fingers until you have breadcrumbs (or whizz in a food processor).

4 Stir together the milk, vanilla and lemon in a measuring jug, then pour into the mixing bowl.

5 Mix until you have a dough, then leave to sit for 5 minutes.

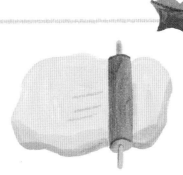

6 On a lightly floured surface, roll out the dough until it is 1cm thick.

7 Cut out 4 scones using a 5cm biscuit cutter and 4 scones using a 6cm biscuit cutter, then transfer to the baking tray.

8 Bake for 15 minutes, until just golden, then allow to cool on a cooling rack.

9 Beat together the icing sugar, water and vanilla until you have a thick icing.

10 Dip the top of a 5cm scone into the icing, then a 6cm scone. Place them next to each other to make a snowperson.

11 Add currants for the eyes, mouth and buttons to finish.

12 Repeat steps 10 and 11 to make the rest of your snowpeople, transfer to plates, then serve.

Top tip: if you don't have biscuit cutters, shape the dough with your hands.

Ingredients

220g plain flour (plus
    extra for dusting)
15g cocoa powder
½ tsp ground cinnamon
A pinch of salt
60g soft brown sugar
120g unsalted butter (cold)
60ml semi-skimmed milk
20 hard-boiled sweets

Makes 30 biscuits

Stained-glass biscuits

These biscuits look so pretty, especially if you hold them up to
the light. For this recipe, I've suggested using a circular biscuit
cutter as well as a heart-shaped cutter for the centres, but you
can use whatever cutters you like. These biscuits are a great
present to give to your best friend. Just wrap a few up in a little
baking paper, tie with a ribbon and add a gift tag. Lovely!

Method

1 Line 2 baking trays with baking paper.

2 In a mixing bowl, toss together the flour, cocoa powder, cinnamon, salt and sugar. Cut the cold butter into small cubes and add to the mixing bowl.

3 Rub together with your fingers until the mixture looks like breadcrumbs.

4 Add the milk, a bit at a time, then squish the mixture until it becomes a dough.

5 Wrap and chill in the fridge for 30 minutes.

6 Unwrap all the boiled sweets of one colour and add to a sandwich bag. Ask an adult to help you crush the sweets into crumbs using a hammer (don't use a wooden rolling pin or board as they could dent).

Top tip: if you don't have biscuit cutters, shape the dough with your hands.

7 Repeat this for different colours in separate bags and set them aside in small bowls.

8 On a lightly floured surface, roll out the dough until it is 0.5cm thick.

9 Cut out discs using an 8cm biscuit cutter, then cut out the centres using a heart-shaped cutter.

10 Add to the baking trays and transfer to the fridge to chill for 20 minutes.

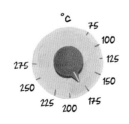

11 Preheat oven to 180°C (fan-assisted).

12 Take the trays out of the fridge and sprinkle the sweet crumbs into the centre of each biscuit.

13 Bake for 10–12 minutes. Allow to cool completely before removing from the baking trays.

Ingredients

Cookies:

60g porridge oats

120g plain flour (plus
    extra for dusting)

40g plain wholemeal flour

½ tsp mixed spice

A pinch of salt

80g unsalted butter

30g smooth peanut butter

70g soft brown sugar

30g runny honey

1 medium egg

Decoration:

1 tbsp cocoa powder

1 tbsp sunflower seeds

1 tbsp poppy seeds

1 tbsp flaked almonds

1 tbsp desiccated coconut

A handful of raisins

6 glacé cherries

Makes 30 biscuits

Family-favourite cookies

Christmas is a time for families to get together. I love making these cookies of my family, and I include all my cousins, aunties and uncles too. I also include my pets! The best part is watching my family try to guess which cookie belongs to each person.

Method

1 Line 2 large baking trays with baking paper.

2 Put the oats in a food processor and blitz until you have a fine powder (or you can leave them whole).

3 Add the flours, mixed spice, salt, butter and peanut butter and blitz until combined.

4 Add the sugar and honey. Crack the egg into the food processor, then pulse everything together until you have a dough.

5 Tip out onto a lightly floured surface and bring together in a ball.

6 Wrap and chill the dough for 1 hour.

7 Add your decorations to little bowls. Ask an adult to help you slice the cherries into small strips.

8 Take a big teaspoonful of biscuit dough, roll in floured hands and press into a face shape.

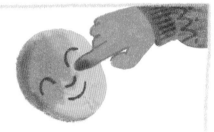

9 Dip your finger in the cocoa powder and pad over the face until you have the correct skin tone.

10 Dip your fingers in water and dab the water along the hairline, then stick on seeds for hair.

11 Press on seeds, nuts or dried fruit to make eyes and noses. You can also use the edge of a spoon to create a smiley mouth, or take blobs of biscuit dough to make other facial features.

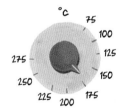

12 Preheat oven to 170°C (fan-assisted).

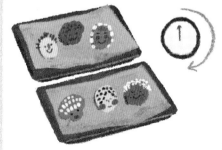

13 Transfer the biscuits to the baking trays and chill in the fridge for 30 minutes.

14 Bake for 15 minutes, then allow to cool for a few minutes before transferring to a cooling rack to cool fully.

Christmas reindeer biscuits

These cookies are clever because you don't need a reindeer cookie cutter to make them. Instead, we use a small gingerbread person cutter and just turn the shape upside down so that it looks like a reindeer's face. Cool, right?

Ingredients

70g butter

30g soft pitted dates

60g icing sugar

15g cocoa powder

½ tsp ground ginger

125g plain flour (plus
    extra for dusting)

2 tsp cold water

100g white chocolate

24 raisins

24 mini pretzels
    (broken into halves)

Makes 24 biscuits

Method

1 Line 2 large baking trays with baking paper.

2 Put the butter and dates in a food processor and blitz until smooth.

3 Add the icing sugar, cocoa powder and ginger and whizz again.

4 Add the flour and pulse a couple of times until mixed through.

5 Add 2 teaspoonfuls of cold water to soften the mixture and pulse again, then tip out onto a surface. Gather up the mixture with your hands until you have a smooth ball of dough.

6 Wrap and chill in the fridge for 30 minutes.

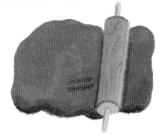

7 On a lightly floured surface, roll out the dough until it is 0.5cm thick.

8 Cut out biscuits using a gingerbread person cutter, no bigger than 10cm tall, and transfer to the baking trays.

9 Chill in the fridge for another 30 minutes.

10 Preheat oven to 160°C (fan-assisted).

11 Bake for 14 minutes, then allow to cool completely on a cooling rack.

12 Break the chocolate into pieces and add to a microwavable bowl. Ask an adult to help you microwave it for 30 seconds, then stir and repeat until it is melted and smooth.

13 Ask an adult to carefully transfer the chocolate to a small piping bag.

14 Pipe blobs of chocolate for the eyes and nose, then place a raisin onto the nose blob.

15 Pipe on ears, then add 2 blobs to the middle of the biscuit. Stick the pretzel antlers onto the blobs, then leave your biscuits to set.

Ingredients

75g unsalted butter

50g caster sugar

100g plain flour (plus
　　extra for dusting)

30g plain wholemeal
　　flour

1 tsp ground cinnamon

1 tsp cocoa powder

1 egg

24 almonds

Makes 24
biscuits

Gifting biscuits

Sometimes baking can be cute, and these biscuits are the cutest! This recipe uses almonds, but you can make the biscuits hold on to whichever type of nut you like. A couple of minutes more or less can make a difference to your biscuits – if you overbake them, they'll be crunchier, and if you underbake them, they'll be soft. Experiment to find your ideal texture and have fun!

Top tip: make a hole in the top point of the biscuit before baking and then hang the baked star on your Christmas tree.

Method

1 Line a large baking tray with baking paper.

2 Ask an adult to melt the butter and sugar together in a small saucepan over a low heat.

3 Toss together the flours, cinnamon and cocoa powder in a mixing bowl.

4 Ask an adult to help you pour over the butter mixture and stir until combined.

5 Crack the egg into the bowl and beat until the batter is thoroughly combined and shiny (don't worry if it looks very wet at this stage).

6 Lay a piece of cling film in another mixing bowl, then pour the biscuit mixture into the middle. Bring the cling film together and twist, then chill the bowl in the fridge for 1 hour.

7 On a lightly floured surface, tip out the dough and roll it out until it is about 0.5cm thick.

8 Cut out stars from the dough using a 7cm star-shaped biscuit cutter. Bring the extra dough together, re-roll and cut out stars until you have 24 biscuits.

9 Place an almond on 1 of the star points on each biscuit, then fold over the point.

10 Using a skewer and the edge of a teaspoon, add eyes and a mouth, then carefully place the biscuits on the lined baking tray. Chill the tray in the fridge for 30 minutes.

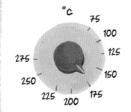

11 Preheat oven to 170°C (fan-assisted).

12 Once the biscuits have chilled, bake them for 12–14 minutes until golden. Allow to cool before serving on a pretty plate.

Ingredients

40g porridge oats

160ml semi-skimmed milk

225g unsalted butter

140g caster sugar

1 tsp vanilla extract

300g plain flour

2 tsp cornflour

A pinch of salt

½ jar of Christmas jam
   (or strawberry jam)

Makes 20 cookies

Christmas thumbprint cookies

I love eating porridge for breakfast, and one time I made too much, so I decided to turn the leftover porridge into cookies! Porridge oats make the cookies really soft, and the jam makes them extra delicious. You can use your special Christmas jam (p. 12), or any leftover strawberry or raspberry jam. Whatever you choose, these soft and crumbly biscuits will taste yummy.

Method

1 Line a large baking tray with baking paper.

2 Add the oats and milk to a small saucepan and gently heat for about 3 minutes, stirring until thick. Alternatively, cook the milk and oats in the microwave for 1 minute.

3 Next, add the porridge, butter, sugar, vanilla, flour, cornflour and salt to a food processor. Whizz until the mixture starts coming together as a dough.

4 The mixture will be very soft, so take big spoonfuls of mixture and blob them onto the baking tray, keeping the cookies at least 2cm apart.

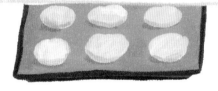

5 Put the tray in the freezer for 30 minutes.

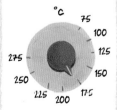

6 Preheat oven to 180°C (fan-assisted).

7 Remove the tray from the freezer, then push your thumb into the middle of each cookie. Fill each thumbprint shape with a teaspoonful of jam.

8 Bake for 20 minutes, or until the cookies just start to turn golden brown. Allow to cool on a cooling rack (the jam will be very hot), then serve.

Festive showstoppers

Christmas igloo cake

Ingredients

Cakes:

75ml vegetable oil

130g caster sugar

100g live natural yogurt

1 medium egg

125g plain flour

2 tsp custard powder

½ tsp baking powder

½ tsp bicarbonate of soda

Decoration:

130g white chocolate

30g desiccated coconut

1 medium egg

180g icing sugar

Makes 9 servings

When I was young, my mum baked cupcakes for me to decorate with my toys and create a scene. Here we make an igloo out of white chocolate and place it on top of iced cupcakes. The royal icing for the cupcakes sets really hard just like a glacier. To make the chocolate igloo, you'll need a balloon, which might seem like a strange idea, but it creates the perfect shape!

Method

1 Break the chocolate into pieces and add to a small microwavable bowl. Ask an adult to help you microwave it for 30 seconds, then stir and repeat until it is melted and smooth.

2 Blow up your balloon until it is about 15–20cm wide. Ask an adult to tie a knot in the balloon, then put the balloon in a bowl with the tied part at the bottom.

3 Once your chocolate is cool, spread it over the top of your balloon, making sure it is evenly coated, then sprinkle with 20g of the coconut.

4 Put the bowl with the chocolatey balloon in the fridge to set (you will need to ask an adult to clear some space).

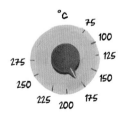

5 Preheat oven to 180°C (fan-assisted).

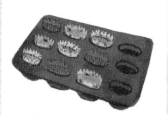  

6 Line a cupcake tray with 9 paper cupcake cases.

7 In a bowl, beat together the oil, sugar and yogurt. Then add the flour, custard powder, bicarbonate of soda and baking powder, mixing until smooth.

8 Divide the mixture between the paper cupcake cases, bake for 15–18 minutes, then leave to cool.

9 To make the icing, crack the egg over a little bowl and let the egg white drip through your fingers, while containing the yolk in your open hand.

10 Beat together the egg white and the icing sugar until smooth.

11 Arrange your cupcakes on a white plate, spread over the icing and sprinkle with the coconut.

12 Take your balloon and carefully turn it upside down. Ask an adult to pop the balloon and remove it from inside the chocolate.

13 Ask them to dip a sharp knife into a cup of boiling water for 10 seconds then carefully cut a little door shape out of the chocolate.

14 Allow the icing to set for at least 3 hours before placing your chocolate igloo on top of your cupcakes.

Ingredients

Bread:

500g strong white bread
flour (plus extra for
dusting)

¼ tsp ground turmeric

7g fast-action yeast
(1 sachet)

1 tsp fine salt

300ml warm water

Zest of 1 orange

60g raisins

30g currants

40g candied mixed peel

1 medium egg

Decoration:

120g icing sugar

Juice of 1 orange

30g glacé cherries

20g flaked almonds

Christmas sprinkles

Makes 12 servings

Golden crown bread

The paper crowns you get in Christmas crackers are so fun to wear.
For this recipe, we make a sweet and doughy bread that is shaped like
a crown. It is based on a Portuguese Christmas cake called a *bolo-rei*,
which is a sweet bread that goes beautifully golden when baked.
It's the perfect treat to share together at this special time of year.

Method

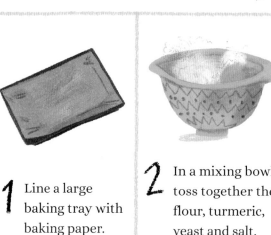

1 Line a large baking tray with baking paper.

2 In a mixing bowl, toss together the flour, turmeric, yeast and salt.

3 Zest the orange and add to a jug of warm water. (Set the orange aside for step 14).

4 Pour the zesty liquid into the mixing bowl and stir until a sticky dough forms.

5 Sprinkle over the dried fruit and mixed peel, then cover and leave to rest for 5 minutes.

6 Knead the bread in the mixing bowl for 5 minutes (do not add extra flour; it doesn't matter if it is a little sticky).

7 Cover and leave to rise in a warm place until it doubles in size (this will take at least 1 hour).

8 On a lightly floured surface, shape the dough into a ball. Push your fingers through the middle, then stretch the bread out until the hole in the middle is about 20cm wide.

9 Place on the baking tray, cover and leave to rise until it doubles in size.

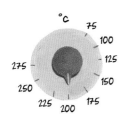

10 Preheat oven to 200°C (fan-assisted).

11 Whisk the egg in a bowl with a fork, then brush the egg onto the bread.

12 Use scissors to make big snips all over the top of the bread.

13 Bake for 25 minutes, then leave to cool on a cooling rack.

14 Squeeze the orange into a bowl and mix 20ml of the juice with the icing sugar.

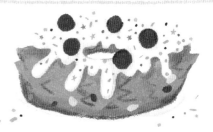

15 Dollop the icing onto the cooled bread, then dot with the cherries, nuts and your Christmas sprinkles.

Ingredients

300g digestive biscuits

100g mini marshmallows

100g dried cranberries

100g raisins

400g chocolate
   (milk or dark)

125g golden syrup

125g unsalted butter

100g white chocolate

Makes 12 servings

Chocolate Christmas pudding

Christmas pudding is one of the most famous Christmas desserts EVER, but lots of people don't like eating it! I have never met anyone who doesn't like rocky road, however. The answer is simple: make a rocky road that looks like a Christmas pudding!

Method

1 Line a small Pyrex bowl (about 18cm wide) with cling film.

2 Put the biscuits in a sandwich bag and gently bash with a rolling pin. You want to break the biscuits into chunks, not into powder, so don't bash them too hard! Add the biscuit chunks to a large mixing bowl.

3 Chop the marshmallows into little cubes and add to the bowl along with the cranberries and raisins.

4 Break the chocolate into pieces and add to a jug or beaker.

5 Ask an adult to help you gently heat the syrup and butter in a saucepan over a low heat, stirring continually until the butter is melted.

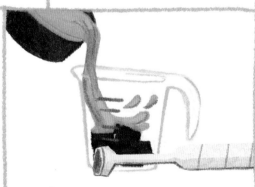

6 Pour the sticky butter mixture over the chocolate and whizz with a hand blender until smooth.

7 Add the chocolate mixture to the mixing bowl and stir until combined.

8 Spoon the rocky road mixture into the lined bowl, then chill it in the fridge for 2 hours.

9 When the chocolate has set, tip the bowl upside down and peel away the cling film.

10 Break the white chocolate into a microwavable bowl. Ask an adult to help you microwave it for 30 seconds, then stir and repeat until it is melted and smooth.

11 Leave to cool for 10 minutes, then ask an adult to help pour the white chocolate carefully over the pudding and top with a clean sprig of holly.

12 Chill your chocolatey pudding in the fridge until everyone is ready to eat it, then ask an adult to carve slices.

Ingredients

Gingerbread:

250g unsalted butter

200g soft brown sugar

80g runny honey

600g plain flour

1 tsp bicarbonate of soda

3 tsp ground ginger

½ tsp ground cinnamon

1 medium egg

Decoration:

350g icing sugar

Flaked almonds

Pumpkin seeds

Raisins, currants,
    cranberries

Small sweets

Chocolate buttons

Makes 8 small
gingerbread houses

Mini gingerbread village

Making a gingerbread house is fun, and the result looks amazing, but sticking the house parts together can be fiddly. Keep going with it and you'll soon have an entire gingerbread village! The key here is to make sure that your icing is thick enough to form a good cement. For this recipe, you'll need a piping bag fitted with a nozzle so that you can pipe decorations around the outsides of the houses.

Method

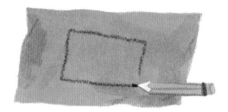

1 Draw a rectangle (about 10cm x 8cm) and a triangle (6cm across and 7cm tall) onto a piece of baking paper, then cut them out. These will be your templates for your gingerbread houses.

2 Line 2–4 large baking trays with baking paper.

3 In a saucepan, gently melt the butter, sugar and honey over a low heat. Remove from the heat and add the flour, bicarbonate of soda and spices.

4 Crack the egg over a bowl and let the egg white drip through your fingers, while containing the yolk in your open hand.

5 Add the yolk to the saucepan and mix the ingredients together until it forms a dough. Keep the egg white for the icing.

6 Lay a large piece of baking paper on a work surface, then tip half of the dough onto it. Lay another piece on top, then roll the dough out until it is 0.5cm thick.

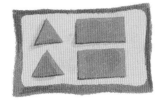

7 Remove the top layer of baking paper, then place your rectangle and triangle templates gently on the dough.

8 Use a blunt knife to carefully cut around the templates so that you have 16 triangles and 16 rectangles.

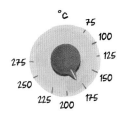

9 Preheat the oven to 180°C (fan-assisted).

10 Put the baking trays in the fridge until the oven is up to temperature.

11 Bake the biscuits for 12–14 minutes, until they are just browning at the edges, then allow to cool fully on the trays.

12 Whisk together the egg white with the icing sugar until you have a smooth, thick icing, then transfer to the piping bag (if too thick, add a teaspoonful of water until ketchup consistency).

13 To make a house, pipe icing along the side edges of 2 triangles and then attach a rectangle on each side. Let the icing set until it goes really hard (this will take at least 2 hours).

14 Once the houses are stuck together, use the remaining icing to pipe on your decorations, sticking on the nuts, seeds, dried fruit, sweets and chocolate.

David Atherton is the winner of *The Great British Bake Off* 2019. David's cookery books for children – *My First Cook Book: Bake, Make and Learn to Cook, My First Green Cook Book: Vegetarian Recipes for Young Cooks* and *My First Baking Book: Delicious Recipes for Budding Bakers* – inspired a generation of children to create healthy, imaginative recipes for their friends and family. David is a food writer and an international health adviser for a charity. He has worked on health programmes around the world and never misses an opportunity to explore a new food culture. David is passionate about ensuring that children grow up as food lovers and understand how to make tasty, healthy food.

Katie Cottle is a Welsh illustrator who now lives in England. Katie has illustrated a number of children's books, and she's written a few too. Katie uses lots of bright colours (orange being a particular favourite), lots of texture and has lots of fun with characters. When she's not drawing, she's probably daydreaming about her future pets or feeding the ducks that live nearby.